FEATHERED FRIENDS

# CROWS

Kim Thompson

NorwoodHouse Press

**Cataloging-in-Publication Data**

Names: Thompson, Kim.
Title: Crows / Kim Thompson.
Description: Buffalo, NY : Norwood House Press, 2027. | Series: Feathered friends | Includes glossary and index.
Identifiers: ISBN 9781978580411 (pbk.) | ISBN 9781978580428 (library bound) | ISBN 9781978580435 (ebook)
Subjects: LCSH: Crows--Juvenile literature.
Classification: LCC QL696.P2367 T548 2027 | DDC 598.864--dc23

Published in 2027 by
**Norwood House Press**
2544 Clinton Street
Buffalo, NY 14224


Designer: Rhea Magaros
Editor: Tricia Hoffman

**Photo credits:** Cover, p.1 F.Demonsant/Shutterstock.com; p.5 Ralph Lear/Shutterstock.com; p.6 Jean Blom/Shutterstock.com; p.7 Matt Krofcheck/Shutterstock.com; p.8 Kevin White Photographer/Shutterstock.com; p.9 knelson20/Shutterstock.com; p.11 KrisDurlen/Shutterstock.com; p.12 Piotr Velixar/Shutterstock.com; p.13 Mr.Teerat/Shutterstock.com; p.15 nambu kim/Shutterstock.com; p.16 An.He/Shutterstock.com; p.18 Audra Thomson/Shutterstock.com; p.19 Rudra Narayan Mitra/Shutterstock.com; p.20 Ron Lam/Shutterstock.com;



Printed in the United States of America



CPSIA compliance information: Batch #CSNHP27: For further information contact Norwood House Press at 1-800-237-9932.

# TABLE OF CONTENTS

## What Do Crows Look Like?

Crows are our feathered friends. These birds are completely black from their **beaks** to their tails. Their glossy feathers look **iridescent** in the sunlight.

Crows can be as long as a bed pillow. They have long legs and thick necks. Their broad wings are rounded at the tips.

Crows are often confused with their relatives, ravens. But ravens are even larger than crows. They have shaggy feathers and pointed wings.

## Where Do Crows Live?

There are many types of crows around the world. American crows live in southern Canada and throughout the United States.

Crows like open areas with trees nearby. Crows can be found in fields, in neighborhoods, and near the ocean.

## How Do Crows Grow Up?

Males and females build nests together. In spring or summer, the female lays four or five eggs. The young leave the nest when they are about five weeks old.

Many crows live in family groups. Hundreds or thousands join in large **flocks**. Together, they **forage** for food and **roost** in trees.

Some crows stay near the place where they were born. They protect the **territory** and help raise babies.

# What Do Crows Eat?

Crows are **omnivores**. They eat whatever they find. They look for insects, worms, fruits, grains, nuts, and the eggs of other birds. They hunt for small animals such as frogs and mice. They feast on roadkill and other **carrion**.

Crows may be some of the smartest animals on Earth. They show how clever they are by using tools. Crows use sticks to poke insects under the ground. To open nuts and clams, they drop them on rocks.

# What Sounds Do Crows Make?

The harsh cry of a crow is called a caw. Loud caws warn that danger is near.

With close family members, crows make softer cooing noises.

## What Funny Things Can Crows Do?

Curious crows sometimes like shiny things. They have been known to steal car keys and other metal objects.

# GLOSSARY

**beaks** (beeks): horny, pointed jaws on birds; bird bills

**carrion** (KER-ee-uhn): rotting, dead meat

**flocks** (flahks): groups of animals of one kind that live, travel, or feed together

**forage** (FOR-ij): to search for food

**iridescent** (ir-uh-DEH-suhnt): having shimmering, rainbow-like colors as in a soap bubble

**omnivores** (AHM-nuh-vorz): animals that eat both plants and meat

**roost** (roost): to gather and settle somewhere to rest or sleep

**territory** (TER-i-tor-ee): an area that is defended by an animal and that often contains the animal's home

# THINKING QUESTIONS

1. Describe a crow's feathers.

2. How are crows and ravens different?

3. Where do American crows live?

4. What do crows eat?

5. How do crows show how smart they are?

# INDEX



# ABOUT THE AUTHOR

Kim Thompson is a writer from Columbus, Ohio. She has written many books for kids. Lots of birds come to her backyard feeder. Her favorites are the showy red cardinals, tiny bright goldfinches, and waddling mallard ducks. Her two cats watch from the window.